"This is a classic example of the kind of book readers worldwide have come to expect from the pen of John MacArthur. Saturated with Scripture, straightforward, and easy to understand, MacArthur's words show what the Bible teaches about sanctification and how it applies both to the individual Christian and to the local church. Christians concerned about the kind of teaching that has resulted in the 'hole in our holiness' will find here much to clarify the issue for them and practical encouragement on walking closely with Christ."

Donald S. Whitney, Professor of Biblical Spirituality, The Southern Baptist Theological Seminary; author, *Spiritual Disciplines for the Christian Life* and *Praying the Bible*

"Sanctification—John MacArthur brings to bear the full force of his pastoral passion on this vital theme! Why? First, because Jesus made it the burden of his prayers for us; Paul insisted it is the will of God for every believer; the author of Hebrews wrote that without it none of us will see the Lord—it is heaven's sine qua non. Second, because we are always in danger of demeaning or ignoring holiness. How many books have you read since you last read one on sanctification? *Sanctification* is a powerful tract for our times—a purposefully short book. You can read it in an hour or two, but its goal is the transformation of the rest of your life."

Sinclair B. Ferguson, Chancellor's Professor of Systematic Theology, Reformed Theological Seminary; Teaching Fellow, Ligonier Ministries

"Justification and sanctification are like the two arms of Jesus Christ by which he embraces us to himself. John MacArthur does a masterful job of showing us how Christ, the Great Shepherd whose Spirit lives in every true spiritual shepherd, earnestly desires for his image to be formed in his beloved people."

Joel Beeke, President and Professor of Systematic Theology and Homiletics, Puritan Reformed Theological Seminary; Pastor, Heritage Reformed Congregation, Grand Rapids, Michigan; author, *Reformed Preaching*

"A seasoned, well-regarded preacher of the gospel offers us a scripturally saturated treatise on sanctification. Simple but not simplistic, short but not shallow, John MacArthur not only explains the Bible's teaching on sanctification but also makes the appropriate, sometimes pointed, applications this current generation needs."

Mark Jones, Pastor, Faith Reformed Presbyterian Church, Vancouver, British Columbia

"MacArthur charges Christians to shine as lights in the midst of this darkened, confused generation. The freedom we have in Jesus Christ is a freedom to serve him as our Master and Lord. Just as he has done throughout his ministry, MacArthur faithfully lifts up God's word. This book pleads for holy, joyful living unto the glory of God."

Chris Larson, President and CEO, Ligonier Ministries

"Clear, inspiring, and with just enough cautions about where the world may have snuck into our theology and, therefore, our lives."

Ed Welch, Faculty and Counselor, Christian Counseling & Educational Foundation

"MacArthur has written a concise and straightforward book to stir up Christians to remembrance of what God teaches concerning how we are to grow as believers. He distinguishes biblical sanctification from other pseudo views on the subject and balances the Christian's position *in Christ* with the Christian's walk *with Christ*. I highly recommend this book to help keep us believing rightly so we can live more Christlike lives."

Stuart W. Scott, Associate Professor of Biblical Counseling, The Southern Baptist Theological Seminary

SANCTIFICATION

SANCTIFICATION

God's Passion for
His People

John MacArthur

WHEATON, ILLINOIS

Sanctification: God's Passion for His People

Copyright © 2020 by John MacArthur

Published by Crossway
           1300 Crescent Street
           Wheaton, Illinois 60187

Cover design: Jordan Singer

Cover painting: Makoto Fujimura

First printing 2020

Printed in the United States of America

Unless otherwise indicated, Scripture quotations are from the ESV® Bible (The Holy Bible, English Standard Version®), copyright © 2001 by Crossway, a publishing ministry of Good News Publishers. Used by permission. All rights reserved.

Scripture references marked PHILLIPS are from *The New Testament in Modern English*, translated by J. B. Phillips © 1972 by J. B. Phillips. Published by Macmillan

All emphases in Scripture quotations have been added by the author.

Trade paperback ISBN: 978-1-4335-6738-4
ePub ISBN: 978-1-4335-6741-4
PDF ISBN: 978-1-4335-6739-1
Mobipocket ISBN: 978-1-4335-6740-7

Library of Congress Cataloging-in-Publication Data

Names: MacArthur, John, 1939- author.
Title: Sanctification : God's passion for his people / John MacArthur.
Description: Wheaton : Crossway, 2020. | Includes index.
Identifiers: LCCN 2019025535 (print) | LCCN 2019025536 (ebook) | ISBN 9781433567384 (trade paperback) | ISBN 9781433567391 (pdf) | ISBN 9781433567407 (mobi) | ISBN 9781433567414 (epub)
Subjects: LCSH: Sanctification. | Sanctification–Biblical teaching.
Classification: LCC BT765 .M225 2020 (print) | LCC BT765 (ebook) | DDC 234/.8–dc23
LC record available at https://lccn.loc.gov/2019025535
LC ebook record available at https://lccn.loc.gov/2019025536

Crossway is a publishing ministry of Good News Publishers.

LB		30	29	28	27	26	25	24	23	22	21	20
15	14	13	12	11	10	9	8	7	6	5	4	3	2	1

To Peter Coeler
A true friend marked by uncommon
humility, generosity, and grace

Contents

1

The Prize of the Upward Call

Scripture says of Christ, "He is able to save to the uttermost those who draw near to God through him, since he always lives to make intercession for them" (Heb. 7:25).

We have a clear window into Christ's continual intercession for his people in John 17. That passage is known as Jesus's high priestly prayer. Its centerpiece is a plea for the sanctification of his disciples: "Sanctify them in the truth; your word is truth. As you sent me into the world, so I have sent them into the world. And for their sake I consecrate myself, that they also may be sanctified in truth" (John 17:17–19). Then Jesus pointedly applies that request not only to the twelve, but also to every Christian in all subsequent generations: "I do not ask for these only, but also for those who will believe in me through their word" (17:20).

The Shepherd Theme in Scripture

That petition reveals the true heart of the good shepherd for his people as clearly as anything in Scripture. "He restores my soul. He leads me in paths of righteousness for his name's sake" (Ps. 23:3). As our shepherd, he is the "Overseer of [our] souls" (1 Pet. 2:25). The Greek word translated "Overseer" in that verse is *episkopos,* a word elsewhere translated "bishop." According to *Thayer's Lexicon,*[1] it refers to "a man charged with the duty of seeing that things to be done by others are done rightly." Christ as the chief shepherd is the overseer, or guardian, of our souls—caring for us, protecting us, leading us, correcting us, and giving us nourishment, all with the ultimate goal of our sanctification.

The English word *pastor* also means "shepherd," of course, and every faithful pastor will have a passion for the holiness of Christ's sheep that mirrors the desire of the Savior.

By the way, the divinely chosen imagery of flocks and shepherds is fitting. God knows his people—all believers—are like sheep in many ways. Sheep are not particularly smart, nor are they adroit at navigating around the pitfalls of their environment. So it's not a particularly flattering comparison. But it is one that Scripture makes repeatedly. "We are his people, and the sheep of his pasture" (Ps. 100:3). Peter urges his fellow elders to "shepherd the flock of God that is among you . . . not domineering over those in your charge, but being examples to the flock" (1 Pet. 5:2–3). He

1. Joseph Henry Thayer, *A Greek-English Lexicon of the New Testament* (New York: American Book Co., 1886), 243.

reminds church leaders of their accountability to the chief shepherd (1 Pet. 5:4).

The Shepherd's Task Is Not Easy

In contrast to the tranquil, untroubled imagery we often see when artists portray flocks in the field, real-life shepherding is hard, messy work. The shepherd's tasks are many and varied. He has to lead and feed the flock, care for injured sheep, seek and rescue lost lambs, ward off predators, stand guard overnight, and tend to the flock's every need. It is a highly demanding task—requiring constant vigilance and care.

Caring for the people of God is likewise an exhausting, never-ending series of wide-ranging duties that would tax any man's skill set. Virtually all pastors will at times be called upon to fill practically every role of service in the church from setup to clean-up. In addition to preaching the word (his central and most important assignment), the pastor is burdened with constant concern for the sheep. As Paul wrote, "Who is weak, and I am not weak? Who is made to fall [into sin], and I am not indignant?" (2 Cor. 11:29). Beyond the spiritual struggles are the tasks. The pastor is asked to officiate at marriages, conduct funerals, offer counseling sessions, make hospital visits, and perform a host of similar functions. A pastor might be faced with wildly disparate duties all in one day—visiting prisoners in the morning and preparing sermons in the afternoon, with a stop in between to comfort a grieving family. He has to be able to move gracefully from one task to another and be skilled at all of them.

Despite the diversity of so many responsibilities, all those pastoral duties ultimately point to one clear and singular goal: the sanctification of God's people. All the man's energies and all the faculties of his heart and mind must remain focused on that one long-range goal, and he must never lose sight of it. This is, after all, God's ultimate purpose for his elect: "For those whom he foreknew he also predestined to be conformed to the image of his Son" (Rom. 8:29). That is how Scripture summarizes the goal of sanctification—not merely to make us *appear* holy, but to make us truly and thoroughly Christlike.

I was struck once more with this great truth while preaching through Galatians 4 recently. I came to verse 19, where Paul addresses the believers of that region as "my little children, for whom I am again in the anguish of childbirth until Christ is formed in you!" That text gripped my mind and my heart to such a degree that it took me a long time to get beyond it. It is a fine summation of every pastor's ministry purpose: to see that Christ is formed in his people.

This of course has significant ramifications not only for pastors and church leaders, but for every Christian as well. Your duty as a believer, no matter who you are, is "to put off your old self, which belongs to your former manner of life and is corrupt through deceitful desires, and to be renewed in the spirit of your minds, and to put on the new self, created after the likeness of God in true righteousness and holiness" (Eph. 4:22–24).

The True Shepherd's Greatest Burden

What struck me afresh about Galatians 4:19 was the passion expressed in the analogy Paul chose. He yearned for the sanctification of his people. He ached to be used of God to spur them on to Christlikeness. And his desire to see the completion of that goal was so deep and so profound that the only apt comparison he could envision was the bittersweet agony of a woman in the pain of giving birth.

That burning passion kept the apostle focused and faithful through a relentless onslaught of vexing trials and persecutions. Here's how Paul recapped his life in ministry. He said he had endured:

> far greater labors, far more imprisonments, with countless beatings, and often near death. Five times I received at the hands of the Jews the forty lashes less one. Three times I was beaten with rods. Once I was stoned. Three times I was shipwrecked; a night and a day I was adrift at sea; on frequent journeys, in danger from rivers, danger from robbers, danger from my own people, danger from Gentiles, danger in the city, danger in the wilderness, danger at sea, danger from false brothers; in toil and hardship, through many a sleepless night, in hunger and thirst, often without food, in cold and exposure. (2 Cor. 11:23–27)

Then he added this: "And, apart from other things, there is the daily pressure on me of my anxiety for all the churches" (11:28).

That the issue of sanctification—holiness—weighed so heavily on the heart of the apostle is a fitting reminder to pastors and church members alike that we must not forget what God is doing with us. "He chose us in him before the foundation of the world, that we should be holy and blameless before him" (Eph. 1:4). It is our duty as believers "to put on the new self, created after the likeness of God in true righteousness and holiness" (4:24). God is conforming us to the likeness of his dear Son. Even our bodies will ultimately be resurrected and glorified to be like the risen Christ (Phil. 3:21). "Just as we have borne the image of the man of dust, we shall also bear the image of the man of heaven" (1 Cor. 15:49).

That goal cannot be thwarted nor the progress ever permanently stopped. True believers will one day be completely perfected. "Beloved, we are God's children now, and what we will be has not yet appeared; but we know that when he appears we shall be like him, because we shall see him as he is" (1 John 3:2).

The finish line may appear to be so far in the distance that it's tempting to give up. The apostle Paul acknowledged that he too felt that frustration: "Wretched man that I am! Who will deliver me from this body of death?" (Rom. 7:24). But he did not quit: "I press on to make it [i.e., the goal of complete sanctification] my own, because Christ Jesus has made me his own. Brothers, I do not consider that I have made it my own. But one thing I do: forgetting what lies behind and straining forward to what lies ahead, I press on toward the goal for the prize of the upward call of God in Christ Jesus" (Phil. 3:12–14).

That's how we must live. And in the pages that follow, we'll consider why this is such a dominant priority.

2

In Defense of the Gospel

Paul, an ultraorthodox Jew, Pharisaical legalist, rising star among Israel's religious elite, persecutor of Christians, ruthless and relentless enemy of the church, was suddenly converted to Christ on the Damascus Road. Paul had always been the most fastidious of Pharisees. Like everyone else in that strict, authoritarian cult of religious partisans, he had an obsession with flashy but trivial symbols of external piety—showy rituals, raiment, and other forms of religious trumpery. His notion of sin was likewise focused on external and trivial things—and (like all hypocrites) he was chiefly concerned about other people's sins. He had a particular contempt for things deemed ceremonially unclean, including (of course) Samaritans and Gentiles. But after Paul's conversion, Christ called him to be an apostle to those "unclean" Gentiles—and his contempt was directed toward real sin.

Paul still had a heart for Israel—such a passion for their salvation that he said, "I could wish that I myself were accursed and cut off from Christ for the sake of my brothers, my kinsmen according to the flesh" (Rom. 9:3). God gave him a love for Gentiles too, and then sent him to evangelize in Gentile regions all around the Roman Empire. Paul went first into the southern part of Galatia and planted churches in Antioch, Iconium, Derbe, and Lystra. That area was not far from his family home in Tarsus of Cilicia. But Paul was not content to confine the gospel to one precinct. He planted predominantly Gentile churches across the Mediterranean region on three long missionary journeys.

When problems arose in those churches or Paul's wisdom was sought, he wrote letters back to them as their founding pastor and trusted shepherd. He wrote, of course, with apostolic authority, the very words of God, as he was directed by the Holy Spirit. Most of his epistles to churches and church leaders are inspired Scripture. The apostle Peter expressly acknowledged that (2 Pet. 3:15).

The Galatian Problem

Paul's first divinely inspired letter was probably his epistle to the Galatians, written about AD 49, soon after the Jerusalem Council. That council, as recorded in Acts 15, was convened to discuss the very same issue that was troubling the Galatians. Namely, if faith is the sole instrument of justification—if (as Jesus said) "whoever *believes* in [Christ] is not condemned" (John 3:18); if "whoever *believes* in the Son has eternal life" (3:36); and if whoever hears the gospel and *believes* "does not come into judgment, but has passed from death to life" (5:24)—what then is the role of Old Testament ceremonial law under the new covenant? Specifically, are believing Gentiles obliged to be circumcised and obey the priestly and ceremonial aspects of the Mosaic covenant?

Both Colossians and Hebrews also deal with that question, and both point out that much of Moses's law entailed types and shadows—symbolic features that prefigured Christ. Now that Christ has come, Scripture says those ordinances no longer serve the purpose for which they were given. Specifically, this means that new-covenant believers are no longer bound by the laws and precepts governing ceremonial cleanness, dietary restrictions, Jewish holidays, or matters germane to the temple priesthood, ritualism, and other distinctly Jewish ordinances. Those things were "but a shadow of the good things to come instead of the true form of these realities" (Heb. 10:1; cf. 8:5). Indeed, not only were the ceremonies and symbols contained in the law merely "a shadow of the things to come, *but the substance belongs to Christ*" (Col. 2:17). So how could the ceremonial ordinances be obligatory for Gentiles who were already united with Christ by faith? Was salvation incomplete without the believer's own obedience to the ceremonial features of the Mosaic covenant? Did Gentiles need to be circumcised and keep kosher in order to be saved?

That was the question the Jerusalem Council considered in Acts 15. The faction who opposed Paul's teaching in that council were "believers who belonged to the party of the Pharisees"—former Pharisees, like Paul, who had professed faith in Christ. But these men lacked either clarity or conviction regarding the gospel. They "rose up and said, 'It is necessary to circumcise them and to order them to keep the law of Moses'" (Acts 15:5). In effect, they were saying that faith in Christ is not enough; in order to be justified, Gentiles also need to undergo circumcision and then adhere to all the external ceremonies, rituals, social restraints, and dietary restrictions set forth in the law of Moses. In other words, they were saying that the vestibule into Christianity leads through Judaism, so in order to become Christians, Gentiles must first become Jewish proselytes.

That same doctrine was being disseminated by false teachers among the mostly Gentile churches in Galatia, and believers in those churches were confused. So Paul wrote what is likely his earliest canonical epistle to address that specific issue. The book of Galatians is a fierce defense of faith alone as the sole instrument of justification—the principle of *sola fide.*

The Heart of the Gospel

That believers are justified through faith alone—apart from any meritorious works of their own—is without doubt the central precept of gospel truth. In fact, understood correctly, the doctrine of justification either presupposes or necessitates every other cardinal doctrine. For example, every aspect of Jesus's incarnation is essential to a proper understanding of how believers are justified, because Christ had to be both truly God and truly human in order to be both our great high priest and the perfect sacrifice for our sin (Heb. 2:10–18). "There is one mediator between God and men, the man Christ Jesus" (1 Tim. 2:5). You can't deny the deity or the humanity of Christ and maintain a proper view of justification.

So the doctrine of justification is not only essential to a right understanding of the gospel; it is the doctrine that ties all other cardinal truths together. John Calvin spoke of justification as the principal hinge of all religion. Martin Luther said it is the doctrine by which the church stands or falls.

The apostle Paul clearly had a similar perspective. He had an obvious affection for the doctrine of justification, because he brings it front and center every time he deals with doctrinal matters. In every one of his New Testament epistles he explains this doctrine, defends it, defines it, illustrates it, or otherwise gives it a high level of prominence.

No wonder. Paul knew from bitter experience the futility of Pharisaical legalism and the hopeless spiritual bondage all such works-based religions foster. The apostle had come to deplore asceticism and man-made precepts. That brand of "spirituality" is designed to give the appearance, but not the reality, of holiness. It invariably places followers under a regimen of restrictions that say, "'Do not handle, Do not taste, Do not touch' (referring to things that all perish as they are used)" (Col. 2:21–22). Such rules, Paul says, "have indeed an *appearance* of wisdom in promoting self-made religion and asceticism and severity to the body, but they are of no value in stopping the indulgence of the flesh" (2:23).

When false teachers came to Galatia and began to press believers with that style of legalism, they no doubt were claiming that Jewish ceremonial and dietary customs were necessary for authentic holiness. They surely would have cited Old Testament texts where circumcision, various kinds of abstinence, and other symbolic and sacerdotal observances were commanded. So they *seemed* to have biblical support for their doctrines. But by resurrecting the types and shadows of old-covenant life and making them obligatory features of church life, they were trying to saddle new-covenant believers with a yoke of bondage Christ had already removed. And in the process, they fatally corrupted the gospel. Paul described their doctrine as "a different gospel" (Gal. 1:6); "a gospel contrary to the one we preached to you" (1:8–9).

An Apostolic Anathema

So he wrote an epistle to be circulated first among the Galatian congregations, and it has one clear purpose: to defend the gospel against a legalistic message. It is a powerful defense. The depth of Paul's concern is seen in how speedily he gets to the point. Unlike all his other epistles, Paul does not begin with any words of praise or appreciation for the people in those churches. After the address and a simple greeting where he praises God (1:1–5), he launches into a rebuke:

> I am astonished that you are so quickly deserting him who called you in the grace of Christ and are turning

to a different gospel—not that there is another one, but there are some who trouble you and want to distort the gospel of Christ. But even if we or an angel from heaven should preach to you a gospel contrary to the one we preached to you, *let him be accursed.* As we have said before, so now I say again: If anyone is preaching to you a gospel contrary to the one you received, *let him be accursed.* For am I now seeking the approval of man, or of God? Or am I trying to please man? If I were still trying to please man, I would not be a servant of Christ. For I would have you know, brothers, that the gospel that was preached by me is not man's gospel. For I did not receive it from any man, nor was I taught it, but I received it through a revelation of Jesus Christ. (1:6–12)

The phrase "let him be accursed" is a single word in the Greek text, and a fierce one: *anathema.* Under the inspiration of the Holy Spirit, Paul was pronouncing damnation on anyone who preached a different gospel. And in this context, the false gospel he was concerned with is the legalism of those who were blending the idea of meritorious works with faith in Christ as the precondition for justification, thus making the sinner's own legal obedience a requirement for salvation.

Again, these legalists no doubt claimed (and perhaps foolishly believed) that they were promoting holiness. In reality, they were undermining the true sanctification of believers in Galatia and promoting a false notion of what holiness entails.

The legalists seemed to believe that the principle of *sola fide* was hostile to holiness. In Romans 6, Paul himself acknowledges how easy it would be for a careless or superficial thinker to draw that conclusion: "What shall we say then? Are we to continue in sin that grace may abound?" (Rom. 6:1). "Are we to sin because we are not under law but under grace?" (6:15).

But Paul quickly and emphatically refutes those suggestions: "By no means!" (6:15). "How can we who died to sin still live in it?" (6:2). "Having been set free from sin, [we] have become slaves of righteousness" (6:18). For Paul, the doctrine of justification by faith is a powerful *incentive* to holiness.

Paul's concern for the Galatians was twofold. First, he was deeply troubled that they were so easily being seduced away from the clarity and simplicity of the true gospel as he himself had brought it to them (Gal. 1:6). But alongside that, he was profoundly concerned for their sanctification. They were being drawn off course, lured into a Pharisaical form of strict externalism, putting themselves under bondage to the very threat of condemnation they had been redeemed from, adopting a system that was guaranteed to breed self-righteousness, and thus forfeiting the goal of true Christlikeness.

That concern is what prompted Paul's lament in Galatians 4:19–20: "My little children, for whom I am again in the anguish of childbirth until Christ is formed in you! . . . I am perplexed about you."

3

The Heart of a True Shepherd

The Galatians were true believers, and therefore Paul addresses them as spiritual children (4:19)—and as "brothers" (4:12, 28, 31). He writes, "You are sons. . . . You have come to know God, or rather to be known by God" (4:6, 9). Clearly he does not regard them as unbelievers. Yet he says, "I am afraid I may have labored over you in vain" (4:11).

Foolish Believers?

Galatians 3 begins with a harsh rebuke that would probably sound like he regards them as heretics or cultists if it were not for all those occasions where Paul affirms their conversion and refers to them as brethren. He writes:

> O foolish Galatians! Who has bewitched you? It was before your eyes that Jesus Christ was publicly portrayed as crucified. Let me ask you only this: Did you receive the Spirit by works of the law or by hearing with faith?

Are you so foolish? Having begun by the Spirit, are you now being perfected by the flesh? Did you suffer so many things in vain—if indeed it was in vain? Does he who supplies the Spirit to you and works miracles among you do so by works of the law, or by hearing with faith? (3:1–5)

He uses the word *foolish* twice. Of course, Jesus forbids us to use such language when the purpose is merely to insult. "Whoever insults his brother will be liable to the council; and whoever says, 'You fool!' will be liable to the hell of fire" (Matt. 5:22). But when some vital spiritual principle is at stake and a brother is being sinfully obtuse, such an expression may in fact be warranted. Jesus himself used similar language about his own disciples in Luke 24:25: "O foolish ones, and slow of heart to believe all that the prophets have spoken!" Clearly, true believers *can* at times be fools and slow of heart.

Paul even raises the possibility that whatever persecution or suffering they had endured was all in vain. It becomes an extended reprimand, and he punctuates the whole admonition in Galatians 4:20 with this: "I wish I could be present with you now and change my tone, for I am perplexed about you."

Still, even in that passage at the start of chapter 3, right where he begins his most harsh and direct chiding of the Galatian believers themselves, Paul makes it clear that—as perplexed as he is, as frustrated as he might be about their openness to a different gospel—he still regards them as true believers. They have seen the revelation of Jesus Christ (3:1); they have experienced the power of the Holy Spirit (3:5); and they have been blessed by the Father (3:8–9). In other words, by trying to adjust the gospel, these false teachers were denying the work of Father, Son, and Holy Spirit. This was an all-out assault on heaven.

That's what the false teachers were guilty of, and Paul did not hold anything back in his criticism of them. The Galatians were Paul's own spiritual children, and that is why he was so grieved and perplexed about their spiritual instability. Though he used severe language, he seasoned it with grace. He reminds them that they began in the Spirit (3:3). Furthermore, Paul says, "In Christ Jesus you are all sons of God, through faith" (3:26). "If you are Christ's, then you are Abraham's offspring, heirs according to promise" (3:29). A chapter later, he adds, "You, brothers, like Isaac, *are* children of promise" (4:28).

And yet he levels this stunningly harsh rebuke at them in the opening verses of chapter 3: "O foolish Galatians! Who has bewitched you?" Here's how J. B. Phillips paraphrased that verse: "O you dear idiots of Galatia. . . . Surely you can't be so idiotic" (PHILLIPS). *Are you deluded? How can you be so stupid?*

Bewitched Christians?

He suggests that they might have been "bewitched." Not only can believers sometimes be foolish; they are also susceptible to being beguiled by false teaching. Can an entire church (or group of churches) be bewitched? That's precisely what Paul indicates here. (I might go so far as to say that I wonder sometimes if *most* churches today are bewitched.)

Paul uses a Greek verb, *baskainō*, that is used nowhere else in Scripture. It means "to allure," or "to charm." But the term always connotes evil intent on the part of the person performing the action. *Baskainō* can refer to deception gained by flattery. *Thayer's Lexicon* includes this definition: "to bring evil on one by feigned praise or an evil eye, to charm, bewitch."[1] The word is frequently used in ancient secular literature to speak of demon spells, curses, incantations, and sorcery. "Bewitched" is a good translation, and it fits the tone of Paul's frustration.

He raises a similar question in milder terms in Galatians 5:7: "You were running well. Who hindered you from obeying the truth?" Notice that their sanctification is what was being severely hindered, or interrupted. They were being charmed in a deceitful way, and it was leading them away from authentic holiness.

So the apostle tells them they were assaulting heaven by tolerating the lie that works are necessary for justification. Consequently, they were confused—spiritually and intellectually blinded as if a spell had been put on them—and their sanctification was in a stagnant state.

Bewitched is not merely a cold, analytical term; it's full of passion. And it was no accident that Paul chose that word. He saw the false teachers' deception as a deeply sinister

---

1. Joseph Henry Thayer, *A Greek-English Lexicon of the New Testament* (New York: American Book Co., 1886), 98.

threat to the one ultimate purpose every legitimate pastor has for being in the ministry—to be an agent for his people's sanctification. And Paul's passion comes through clearly as he confronts and corrects the error.

The apostle was vexed and outraged by the threat of a different gospel. He was equally dismayed and heartbroken by the lack of settled conviction in the Galatian congregations. These were people he knew and had led to Christ. How could they be seduced so easily by false teachers who obviously had no respect for the apostle?

A Loving, Self-Sacrificial Shepherd

The whole stunning range of emotion is vividly expressed in this letter. Paul's heart is burning, and he wants the Galatians to know it. In a manner not typical for him, he writes repeatedly about how he feels. He expressly says he is astonished (1:6); he is indignant (1:8–9); he is in anguish (4:19); he is fearful (4:11); he is perplexed (4:20). It is obvious also that he feels attacked, offended, and indignant toward the false teachers. He is exasperated, he is condemnatory, he is confrontive, he is sarcastic, he is severe, he is dogmatic, he is demanding, he is hurt, and he is humbled. That is a wide range of negative distress. But at the same time, it is clear that he is loving, devoted, obedient, confident, encouraging, sacrificial, protective, faithful, and hopeful.

That, by the way, is the world every pastor lives in *if he cares about the sanctification of his people.* Those will all be familiar feelings for anyone serving in church ministry—

except, perhaps, for those who have selfish goals—rather than wanting to see their people grow and mature in Christlikeness.

Sadly, there are many in positions of church leadership today who occupy the pulpit for purely self-aggrandizing reasons. They may be motivated by greed, conceit, carnal ambition, a lust for money and power, or a desire for honor and applause. They preach themselves rather than Christ Jesus as Lord (cf. 2 Cor. 4:5). They exploit people rather than serve them (2 Pet. 2:3). And sometimes they are surprisingly crass and candid about their real objectives. I've cataloged some of the popular words pastors today like to use as self-descriptors. None of these words would ever have been used by Paul to describe his ministry. But they are commonly employed today, not only in pastoral resumés but also in the want ads from churches seeking pastors. These adjectives therefore describe what many young men entering ministry today aspire to be. They have been told, and firmly believe, that in order to thrive in the ministry, they must be *relevant, authentic, always agreeable, acclaimed, innovative, cool, contemporary, creative, clever, culturally savvy, fashionable, inclusive, imaginative, broad-minded, visionary, unconventional, iconoclastic, entertaining, extreme, woke*—or some combination of those qualities.

Self-congratulatory adjectives like those constitute the lingo of pastoral ministry nowadays. I saw the publicity for a church leadership conference not long ago whose organizers gave themselves the title "Hero Makers." Words typically missing from all those want ads, promotional pieces, and resumés are: biblical, holy, humble, godly, separated, self-denying, pure, faithful, sacrificial, and sanctified.

When Paul wrote Galatians with such a wide range of intense passions, he was not having a temporary psychological burnout or midlife crisis. Those same affections would occupy his heart throughout his entire ministry. About six years after writing Galatians, he wrote to the church at Corinth:

> I wish you would bear with me in a little foolishness. Do bear with me! For I feel a divine jealousy for you, since I betrothed you to one husband, to present you as a pure virgin to Christ. But I am afraid that as the serpent deceived Eve by his cunning, your thoughts will be led astray from a sincere and pure devotion to Christ. For if someone comes and proclaims another Jesus than the one we proclaimed, or if you receive a different spirit from the one you received, or if you accept a different gospel from the one you accepted, you put up with it readily enough. (2 Cor. 11:1–4)

That is essentially the same concern he expressed to the Galatians. The Corinthians were similarly bewitched by false teachers, and, like the Galatians, they were being enticed away from the teaching of Paul (whom they knew and ought to have trusted) by the crafty subterfuge of "false apostles, deceitful workmen, disguising themselves as apostles of Christ" (11:13). These were men whom they had no reason whatsoever to believe.

This is the context where Paul gives a long catalogue of his sufferings (beatings, imprisonments, shipwrecks, assaults, dangers, toil, hardship, sleeplessness, and deprivation) and then adds, "Apart from other things, there is the daily pressure on me of my anxiety for all the churches" (11:28).

He's not talking about administrative headaches. His concern is not about the budget. He immediately gets specific about the nature of the burden he bore: "Who is weak, and I am not weak? Who is made to fall, and I am not indignant?" (11:29).

That is the heart of a true shepherd. If people in his church are led into sin or fall into some transgression, he bears the pain of it. That's how deep the zeal for sanctification is in a faithful pastor's heart.

Paul furthermore tells the Corinthians: "Here for the third time I am ready to come to you. And I will not be a burden, for I seek not what is yours but you. For children are not obligated to save up for their parents, but parents for their children. I will most gladly spend and be spent for your souls" (2 Cor. 12:14–15). That reflects the very same passion Paul always had for the sanctification of his people.

About ten years later he would write to the church at Ephesus, and there he again makes clear what should be the central focus and singular goal of every church leader. He says Christ "gave the apostles, the prophets, the evangelists, the shepherds and teachers, to equip the saints for the work of ministry, for building up the body of Christ, until we all attain to the unity of the faith and of the knowledge of the

Son of God, to mature manhood, to the measure of the stature of the fullness of Christ" (Eph. 4:11–13). Paul saw his task clearly. His role was to participate in leading believers to Christlikeness. That is what he was most passionate about.

He continues the same theme in verses 15–16: "We are to grow up in every way into him who is the head, into Christ, from whom the whole body, joined and held together by every joint with which it is equipped, when each part is working properly, makes the body grow so that it builds itself up in love."

He gave a similar picture of his ministry priorities to the Colossians: "Him [Jesus] we proclaim, warning everyone and teaching everyone with all wisdom, that we may present everyone mature in Christ. For this I toil, struggling with all his energy that he powerfully works within me" (Col. 1:28–29). That was his passion, and that was his purpose—the sanctification of the redeemed whom God had entrusted to his care.

4

Christ, the Embodiment of True Sanctification

The apostle Peter, of course, spent three years during Christ's earthly ministry being personally instructed by the Lord. He was the de facto leader of the twelve—the most outspoken and inquisitive, and by any measure the dominant voice in the group. In a poignant scene on the shores of Galilee after the resurrection, Christ personally commissioned Peter for ministry three times in quick succession. (It was the same number of times Peter had emphatically denied Jesus on the night of his arrest.) Our Lord then forgave him, restored him, and made clear Peter's assignment with the simplest, most direct words possible: "Feed my lambs" (John 21:15); "Tend my sheep" (21:16); "Feed my sheep" (21:17).

So the priority of Peter's ministry was established by Christ himself, and Peter not only got the message; he passed it along to everyone in a position of church leadership under his oversight and beyond. Writing to Jewish believers who had been scattered throughout the empire after the destruction of Jerusalem, he said:

> I exhort the elders among you, as a fellow elder and a witness of the sufferings of Christ, as well as a partaker in the glory that is going to be revealed: *shepherd the flock of God* that is among you, exercising oversight, not under compulsion, but willingly, as God would have you; not for shameful gain, but eagerly; not domineering over those in your charge, but being examples to the flock. And when the chief Shepherd appears, you will receive the unfading crown of glory. (1 Pet. 5:1–4)

How Paul Received the Gospel

But where did the apostle Paul learn that this was to be his priority as well? After all, he had no earthly mentor. Indeed, he made a major point of reminding everyone that he did not derive what he knew of Christ from any secondhand sources. He didn't learn the gospel (much less the character of his ministry) from the other apostles. He says, "The gospel that was preached by me is not man's gospel. For I did not receive it from any man, nor was I taught it" (Gal. 1:11–12). Describing those days immediately after his conversion on the road to Damascus, he says, "I did not immediately consult with anyone; nor did I go up to Jerusalem to those who were apostles before me, but I went away into Arabia, and returned again to Damascus. Then after three years I went up to Jerusalem to visit Cephas and remained with him fifteen days. But I saw none of the other apostles except James the Lord's brother" (1:16–19).

Incidentally, although "James the Lord's brother" became a leader in the early church, he was not one of the twelve either. James *the son of Zebedee* was one of the twelve and became an apostle. (He was the elder brother of the apostle John). But *the apostle* James was killed by Herod shortly after Paul's conversion (Acts 12:2)—before Paul could have possibly met with him. The James whom Paul met on that visit to Jerusalem was the first of four half-brothers of Jesus who are named in Matthew 13:55 and Mark 6:3. All four of Jesus's brothers were unbelievers (John 7:5), and apparently they remained unbelievers until after the resurrection, when we see them in the upper room with the rest of the disciples (Acts 1:14). During those years of Christ's earthly ministry, even when practically everyone else in Galilee was fascinated with Jesus, our Lord's own family thought he was "out of his mind" (Mark 3:21). So Christ's brother James was apparently a latecomer to faith, much like Paul. James wasn't the source of Paul's understanding of the gospel and its ramifications.

Who then discipled Paul? Who revealed the gospel to him with all its vital facts and doctrines, and who appointed and taught him to be an apostle? Paul is emphatic in saying it was Jesus himself. He writes, "I received it through a revelation of Jesus Christ" (Gal. 1:12). He gives no detailed account of how this revelation came to him. It may have been during the experience (possibly a series of experiences) that he mentions in 2 Corinthians 12:2, where he says he was "caught up to the third heaven—whether in the body or out of the body I do not know, God knows."

What Paul *did* know and affirmed categorically was that Christ himself was the one who commissioned him for ministry. And in Paul's own words, this was "in order that I might preach him among the Gentiles" (Gal. 1:16). In 1 Corinthians 15 Paul enumerates hundreds of people who saw the risen Christ with their own eyes, and at the end of the list he includes himself: "Last of all, as to one untimely born, he appeared also to me" (1 Cor. 15:8). So the revelation and training he speaks of in Galatians 1 evidently came through a face-to-face encounter, or a sequence of them.

For the other disciples, the proof that Paul wasn't lying about getting the gospel directly from Christ was clear in the fact that what Paul learned from Jesus was both thorough and in perfect accord with what the Lord had privately taught them. It was the same gospel and the same approach to ministry.

Fourteen years after that first visit to Jerusalem Paul visited again (probably on the occasion of the council described in Acts 15). Paul says the key apostles and leaders in the Jerusalem church "added nothing to me" (Gal. 2:6)—meaning they did not need to correct or amend his account of the Christian message. The doctrine he taught was precisely what they had heard with their own ears from Christ. Paul's ministry and message were exactly the same as Peter's. Therefore, Paul says, when they saw that I had been entrusted with the gospel to the uncircumcised, just as Peter had been entrusted with the gospel to the circumcised (for he who worked through Peter for his apostolic ministry to the circumcised worked also through me for mine to the Gentiles), and when James and Cephas and John, who seemed to be pillars, perceived the grace that was given to me, they gave the right hand of fellowship to Barnabas and me, that we should go to the Gentiles and they to the circumcised. (2:7–9)

How Paul's Ministry Priorities Were Established

The Lord obviously made clear to Paul his passion for the sanctification of believers. Bear in mind that the very centerpiece of Jesus's prayer as our great high priest is an earnest, urgent plea for our sanctification. Consider the larger context of that prayer request.

It is the night of Jesus's betrayal. John 18:4 tells us Jesus knew absolutely everything that was about to happen to him. He fully understood what an unimaginably fearsome price he would pay for the sins of his people, and naturally he dreaded it. Remember how he prayed for himself that night in Gethsemane. He was in excruciating agony—literally sweating blood. Yet he declared his heartfelt willingness to do the Father's perfect will. He nevertheless also expressed a perfectly human wish to avoid, if possible, the cup of wrath he would be asked to drink on behalf of his chosen ones. The magnitude of the burden on his heart that night was such that the depth of his soul's affliction can hardly be described in any human language. He did not exaggerate when he told Peter, James, and John, "My soul is very sorrowful, even to death" (Matt. 26:38).

And yet before he made that prayer for himself, he prayed for his own. The prayer of John 17 took place that same evening just after they had shared the Passover meal together, and immediately before Jesus went to Gethsemane. Judas had already left the gathering to sell Jesus for the price of a slave—thirty pieces of silver—and Jesus clearly understood what Judas was up to (John 13:21–30). With so much weighing on our Lord's heart and mind, although he was obviously eager to get to the garden where he could pray virtually alone in utter agony, it is significant that he stopped to pray aloud (in the hearing of the eleven remaining disciples) the prayer recorded in John 17.

He lifts his eyes to heaven and says a long prayer *for them*—not for everyone indiscriminately, but specifically for the disciples. "I am praying for them. I am not praying for the world but for those whom you have given me, for they are yours" (John 17:9). And as we noted at the start, this prayer is not only for the twelve but for all the elect of all coming generations. "I do not ask for these only, but also for those who will believe in me through their word" (17:20).

Now look at his specific requests. After rehearsing in detail how he has faithfully fulfilled the mission he was given in his incarnation (17:1–11), he enumerates his requests for his people. He prays for their preservation and for unity among them: "Keep them in your name, which you have given me, that they may be one, even as we are one" (17:11). He expresses a desire to see his joy fulfilled in them (17:13). And he asks the Father to keep them from the evil one (17:15).

Each of those requests actually amplifies and expounds on the theme of the whole prayer—namely the request of verse 17: "Sanctify them in the truth; your word is truth."

For example, the prayer for spiritual unity is a thread that runs through the whole chapter. Jesus makes that request repeatedly, praying again and again "that they may all be one, just as you, Father, are in me, and I in you, that they also may be in us" (17:21); "that they may be one even as we are one" (17:22); and "that they may become perfectly one" (17:23). Such unity is possible only among sanctified disciples. So implicit in the request for believers' spiritual unity is the plea for their sanctification. The same thing is true regarding their joy, their preservation, and their Christlike love. All of those things are necessary expressions of true holiness. The entire prayer therefore reflects the priority of sanctification as Christ's will for his people.

Notice also that in every phase of the prayer, Christ himself is the model of what he wants his people to be: "They are not of the world, just as I am not of the world" (17:14, 16). "As you sent me into the world, so I have sent them into the world" (17:18). "For their sake I consecrate myself, that they also may be sanctified in truth" (17:19). "[I ask] that they may be one even as we are one" (17:22). "I desire that they also, whom you have given me, may be with me where I am" (17:24).

Finally, he asks the Father "that the love with which you have loved me may be in them, and I in them" (17:26).

Verse 19 is especially telling. The Lord Jesus Christ in his incarnation sanctified himself (lived in perfect holiness) in order to sanctify his people in the truth. He thus gave us a perfect model to follow. Specifically, "Christ . . . suffered for you, leaving you an example, so that you might follow in his steps. He committed no sin, neither was deceit found in his mouth. When he was reviled, he did not revile in return; when he suffered, he did not threaten, but continued entrusting himself to him who judges justly. He himself bore our sins in his body on the tree, that we might die to sin and live to righteousness" (1 Pet. 2:21–24). In other words, everything he did throughout his earthly life was to set us free from the bondage of sin so that we might become servants of righteousness (Rom. 6:18).

Jesus is the one who taught Paul to pursue sanctification in the power of the Spirit in order that he might be an example and an instrument for the sanctification of the people given into his care. That's how Paul could say, "Be imitators of me, as I am of Christ" (1 Cor. 11:1); "Brothers, join in imitating me" (Phil. 3:17); and "Brothers, I entreat you, become as I am" (Gal. 4:12).

How Paul Passed the Baton

Paul instructed Timothy to embrace a similar role and responsibility for the sake of those in his care: "Set the believers an example in speech, in conduct, in love, in faith, in purity" (1 Tim. 4:12). He further told Timothy to take everything he had learned from Paul and hand it off to qualified, capable men who would carry the baton to the next generation, then hand it off to others who would do the same: "What you have heard from me in the presence of many witnesses entrust to faithful men, who will be able to teach others also" (2 Tim. 2:2).

Scripture speaks on this issue with supreme clarity. Christ's passion for his people's sanctification sets the compass for a sound, biblical philosophy of ministry. This is a priority every competent, biblically qualified church leader will embrace. No one is truly fit to lead the church if he is indifferent about holiness, or if he neglects to instruct and encourage his people in a wholehearted pursuit of sanctification. And, accordingly, every believer must earnestly aspire to grow in grace and Christlikeness with the recognition that this is Christ's constant prayer for—and God's ultimate design for—every believer.

5

The Missing Note

Sanctification is absolutely essential to the life of faith—so much so that Scripture frequently treats holiness as the identifying mark of a true believer. Indeed, when the term *saints* (meaning "holy ones") is used in Scripture, it refers not to dead luminaries whom the church has formally canonized but to living Christians—all the redeemed without exception. Paul writes "to those sanctified in Christ Jesus, called to be saints *together with all those who in every place call upon the name of our Lord Jesus Christ*" (1 Cor. 1:2). Notice that he's not talking about a special class of advanced sainthood. He's underscoring the truth that all genuine believers *are* saints—holy people. A person who is utterly unsanctified is no Christian at all, no matter what verbal confession of faith he or she might make.

God's Will for Every Believer: Sanctification

Accordingly, in Acts 20:32, when Paul uses the expression "all those who are sanctified," he is talking about the church universal. He first heard that expression from Christ himself, on the Damascus road, when he was commissioned as an apostle with these words:

> Rise and stand upon your feet, for I have appeared to you for this purpose, to appoint you as a servant and witness to the things in which you have seen me and to those in which I will appear to you, delivering you from your people and from the Gentiles—to whom I am sending you to open their eyes, so that they may turn from darkness to light and from the power of Satan to God, that they may receive forgiveness of sins and a place among *those who are sanctified by faith in me.* (Acts 26:16–18)

Thus Christ himself described Christians as those who put their faith in him and are thereby made holy. Scripture is equally clear that those who are *unholy*—unrepentant sinners, devoid of any desire for righteousness and lacking any true love for Christ—have no part with him. Real believers "strive . . . for the holiness without which no one will see the Lord" (Heb. 12:14). An unsanctified life is the mark of an unbeliever. The line of demarcation is clear:

> Let no one deceive you. Whoever practices righteousness is righteous, as he is righteous. Whoever makes a practice of sinning is of the devil, for the devil has been sinning from the beginning. The reason the Son of God appeared was to destroy the works of the devil. No one born of God makes a practice of sinning, for God's seed abides in him, and he cannot keep on sinning, because he has been

born of God. By this it is evident who are the children of God, and who are the children of the devil: whoever does not practice righteousness is not of God. (1 John 3:7–10)

Naturally, then, the New Testament is filled with exhortations, instructions, encouragements, commandments, and reminders for believers to strive toward holiness. Despite what you may have heard from the purveyors of popular deeper-life doctrines, we are never encouraged to be passive in the process of sanctification. Scripture does not tell us to "let go and let God." The Bible never promises any easy, automatic victory over sin and temptation.

The notion that sanctification happens with no effort on our part when we passively surrender the fight is a popular, persistent myth—and it's a dangerously false doctrine. In fact, it's the very antithesis of what the Bible teaches. It's reminiscent of the strategic error Moses made when the Israelites arrived at the Red Sea. He told them, "Fear not, stand firm, and see the salvation of the LORD, which he will work for you today. . . . The LORD will fight for you, and you have only to be silent" (Ex. 14:13–14). The Lord responded with a firm word of correction: "Why do you cry to me? Tell the people of Israel to go forward" (14:15).

Similarly, Scripture repeatedly urges Christians to move forward—"press on toward the goal" (Phil. 3:14)—in our quest for holiness: "Beloved, let us cleanse ourselves from every defilement of body and spirit, bringing holiness to completion in the fear of God" (2 Cor. 7:1). "For this is the will of God, your sanctification: that you abstain from sexual immorality; that each one of you know how to control his own body in holiness and honor, not in the passion of lust like the Gentiles who do not know God. . . . For God has not called us for impurity, but in holiness. Therefore whoever disregards this, disregards not man but God, who gives his Holy Spirit to you" (1 Thess. 4:3–8). "Our great God and Savior Jesus Christ . . . gave himself for us to redeem us from all lawlessness and to purify for himself a people for his own possession who are zealous for good works" (Titus 2:13–14). After all, "now that you have been set free from sin and have become slaves of God, the fruit you get leads to sanctification and its end, eternal life" (Rom. 6:22).

The New Testament is replete with exhortations like that. Yet despite the high priority given to the subject by Christ and by Scripture, sanctification is a conspicuously missing emphasis in today's evangelical preaching.

The Young and the Restless

The early years of the twenty-first century have seen a rediscovery and revival of interest in the Protestant Reformation. Young evangelicals have begun to embrace and highlight some of the key doctrines that shaped that movement. They affirm, for example, the principles of *sola fide* (faith as the sole instrument of justification), *sola gratia* (salvation by grace alone, apart from the sinner's own meritorious works), and *solus Christus* (Christ as the only way to God). There has been in recent years an encouraging resurgence of conviction that God is sovereign in the election and salvation of sinners; that (as texts like Acts 11:18; 14:27 indicate) repentance from sin is God's gracious work, not the fruit of the sinner's own free will; and that God truly "works *all* things according to the counsel of his will" (Eph. 1:11). More important is that in the first decade of the new millennium, we saw a renewed emphasis on the doctrines of justification, substitutionary atonement, and the exclusivity of Christ. Those are all core gospel truths. They were not necessarily denied by previous generations of evangelicals, but they were usually taken for granted, and therefore they had been largely ignored for decades.

All the renewed interest in these crucial doctrines has been a good and important development—as far as it went.

The title of a September 2006 article by Collin Hansen in *Christianity Today* gave this trend a nickname that stuck: "Young, Restless, Reformed." The article (later expanded into a book) was published with the subtitle, "Calvinism is making a comeback—and shaking up the church."[1]

But some of the leading figures in the developing movement have not been able to break away from the crass pragmatism that dominated the evangelical movement in their parents' generation. They are obsessed with anything hip or trendy, appropriating the fads and memes of pop culture—and justifying their pragmatism by telling themselves they are redeeming the arts, engaging the culture, contextualizing,

---

1. Collin Hansen, "Young, Restless, Reformed: Calvinism is making a comeback—and shaking up the church, *Christianity Today*, September 22, 2006, accessed August 22, 2019, https://www.christianitytoday.com/ct/2006/september/42.32.html.

being "missional," or being "incarnational." Young, restless evangelicals have a host of pet subjects and tropes like that. *Holiness* does not appear to be one of them, let alone the main one.

That's an approach to reformation that none of the magisterial Reformers or their spiritual heirs would recognize. To call it "Reformed" or regard it as a legitimate expression of Calvinism is an affront to the true history of the Protestant Reformation.

By 2011, beer, cigars, and tattoos had become the de facto emblems of the Young, Restless movement instead of the Reformed doctrines they professed to believe. Their literature, blogposts, podcasts, and sermons seemed barely to mention sanctification—except to dismiss every mention of holiness as a dangerous form of legalism. One well-known pastor in the movement even declared that abstinence from alcoholic beverages is a sin that needs to be repented of. I wrote a blogpost expressing concern about the direction the movement was headed and was derisively lampooned by a large number of leading voices in the movement as a doddering legalist.

My concern was—and still is—that the movement as a whole has stressed and overstated the principle of Christian liberty without the necessary balance. True Christian liberty means deliverance from sin's bondage and the law's condemnation, not freedom from the law's moral precepts. Having been set free from sin and death, we are now called to live as slaves of righteousness (Rom. 6:18). Scripture says, "Live as people who are free, not using your freedom as a cover-up for evil, but living as servants of God" (1 Pet. 2:16). "Now that you have been set free from sin and have become slaves of God, the fruit you get leads to sanctification" (Rom. 6:22). "Do not use your freedom as an opportunity for the flesh" (Gal. 5:13).

Indicatives and Imperatives

Float those ideas in almost any evangelical gathering today and someone will bristle and object. They have been taught that the many *imperatives* (commands) in Scripture are law and therefore they should not be declared to Christians as duties we must obey. After all, we "are not under law but under grace" (Rom. 6:14). Therefore, they say, the Bible's *indicatives* (statements of objective facts) are what we need to pay attention to—reassuring truths such as Romans 8:1: "There is therefore now no condemnation for those who are in Christ Jesus."

Certainly, we should proclaim and emphatically affirm the gospel's indicatives. These generally pertain to our justification: "By grace you have been saved through faith. And this is not your own doing; it is the gift of God, not a result of works" (Eph. 2:8–9).

But when the subject is *sanctification,* the Bible is full of imperatives: "Put off your old self, which belongs to your former manner of life and is corrupt through deceitful desires, and . . . be renewed in the spirit of your minds, and . . . put on the new self, created after the likeness of God in true righteousness and holiness" (Eph. 4:22–24). Ephesians 4 continues with a long list of imperatives that extends well into chapters 5 and 6. Unlike so many today, Paul did not shy away from speaking of sanctification or growth in grace as a duty.

Indeed, as we have seen from the very start, sanctification was Paul's central concern for the Christians of Galatia. He was as earnestly intent on leading them to mature Christlikeness as he had been to bring them to faith in the beginning. He says, "I am *again* in the anguish of childbirth until Christ is formed in you!" (Gal. 4:19). He was in spiritual labor while bringing them to the new birth of regeneration. Now he was feeling all the same agonizing birth pains, laboring to bring them to maturity.

Maturity seems to be in rare supply in churches today. Church leaders—even middle-aged ones—try to dress, talk, and act like adolescents. Multitudes raised in evangelical youth ministries (where the chief goal was to keep them entertained) never learned to think seriously about spiritual matters.

We need to move past the young-and-restless stage. Immaturity and instability are hindrances to spiritual fruitfulness, not virtues. Real holiness makes a person steadfast and mature. Paul wrote, "Brothers, do not be children in your thinking. Be infants in evil, but in your thinking be mature" (1 Cor. 14:20). He described sanctification in precisely these terms: "mature manhood . . . the measure of the stature of the fullness of Christ" (Eph. 4:13).

Let's Pursue True Holiness

Why is this emphasis missing in contemporary evangelical churches? I grew up hearing sermons regularly about the need for holiness, godliness, Christlikeness, separation from sin and from the world and its values. In previous generations, if a preacher neglected the theme of holiness, it would have stood out as a major (and deeply troubling) omission. Calls to godly obedience had a much higher place in the message that came from the pulpit, in the thinking of people in the pews, and in the life of the church as a whole.

Sanctification was a major emphasis in every confessionally Protestant and biblically oriented denomination. And preachers boldly proclaimed the need for sanctification right alongside the doctrine of justification by faith.

Historic Protestants understood that the main work of the Holy Spirit was not to produce bizarre, inexplicable, esoteric, out-of-body phenomena. The real work of the Holy Spirit was seen in manifest holiness—Christlike virtue. No one ever imagined any conflict between the dual truths that believers are saved "through sanctification by the Spirit *and* belief in the truth" (2 Thess. 2:13).

None of that is true anymore. The truth of sanctification, together with words like *holiness, godliness,* and *Christlikeness* are all but gone from popular Christian discourse. Rarely do you hear any popular preachers urge their people to be separate from the world, to deny fleshly desires, or to mortify sin and selfishness. Instead, following the popular strategies of pragmatism and seeker-sensitivity, all the longings of the selfish human heart are being legitimized. The fads and entertainments of the world—along with some of the twisted moral values of the sexual revolution—are being incorporated into churches, because pastors have been told these are necessary elements to attract people who otherwise have no interest in God.

Inexplicably, even many pastors and church leaders who profess to believe that God is sovereign and the gospel is the power of God for salvation have embraced that blatantly pragmatic philosophy. They will say they believe the doctrine of justification by faith, and they don't mind preaching about it from time to time, because they can do it in a way that won't intrude on an unbeliever's comfort zone. They might even occasionally bring up the subject of glorification (though I fear too many preachers are so obsessed with this world and so passionate about connecting with today's "culture" that they rarely look into the eschatalogical future). But practically nothing is said about sanctification. In fact, preaching is designed to make people feel good about the way they are and to assure them that God likes them that way.

It's a new version of Christianity—neither genuinely reformed nor historically Protestant. At best we might call it neo-Reformed.

On the other hand, there is a remnant of faithful churches with faithful ministers—godly shepherds who lead their flocks away from the world, away from self-interest, away from the fulfillment of their own desires, away from seeking and defining life only in terms of their own wish list. That's what every church leader *and* every church member should aspire to. It is always dangerous to let oneself carelessly drift with the mainstream, and it has never been shameful to be part of the remnant. Remember Christ's words about the faithful minority in Sardis: "You have still a few names in Sardis, people who have not soiled their garments, and they will walk with me in white, for they are worthy" (Rev. 3:4).

That is the ultimate prize of our high calling, and it's of infinitely greater value than all the treasures of this world combined. It's the best of all reasons to keep pressing on toward the goal of mature Christlikeness.

6

Authenticity and Antinomianism

How did we get to this point?

Bible-centered, gospel-focused churches for centuries stressed the value of sound theological understanding, the transcendent holiness of God, God-centered and Christ-exalting worship, the true work of the Spirit, spiritual growth, and Christlike virtue—all realities that point to the need for sanctification. Churches opposed worldliness, decried superficiality, rebuked sin, understood the value of sound doctrine, and refuted false doctrines. Worship was praise directed to God for his glory, not a performance suited to the stylistic preferences of the congregation and offered for their entertainment. God is the only audience in true worship.

There were obviously plenty of churches (and even whole denominations) that apostatized, compromised, or otherwise failed to remain sound and committed to those principles. But the biblical standards governing ministry philosophy are not the least bit hazy, ambiguous, or complicated, and there was a general understanding among believers about what a biblical church *should* be like.

That has changed. Multitudes of nominally evangelical churches today are nothing more than psychological, sociological, pragmatic, anthropocentric community centers dressed in religious garb—or something more stylishly casual, like printed T-shirts and grungy, torn blue jeans. They use the name of Jesus as a token, but they believe success or failure hinges on their own cleverness. They measure their effectiveness by attendance figures or money in the offering plate. Their idea of worship is a mindless musical stimulation designed for emotional manipulation of the people rather than praise offered to God. Vague spirituality and nice-sounding platitudes replace biblical doctrine and true holiness. And the focus of the message is personal satisfaction rather than Spirit-empowered sanctification. People attend not because they love the truth and fear God, but because everything they see and hear caters to their love of self.

A Worldly Notion of Authenticity

One of the fundamental errors underlying this drift is an idea borrowed from secular thought. It's traceable back at least to Sigmund Freud, the father of psychoanalysis. Freud believed people need to be free from restraint and free from shame in order to be "authentic." *Authenticity* became a key word in psychology and in virtually all postmodern philosophies.

Being authentic means being true to yourself, and that in turn means embracing the legitimacy of your own desires and inner drives. You are truly authentic when you act accordingly. In other words, be who you are; this is your true self. Any attempt to stifle, suppress, or screen your impulses is seen as insincere and artificial.

This sort of existential authenticity is supposed to be liberating. You can indulge your fundamental urges and salve a troubled heart by convincing your conscience that being true to yourself is the highest virtue.

Obviously, the most authentic souls in the world today are young people who don't have the inhibitions and regret that come with learning the lessons of life. They haven't been subject to the inevitable constraints of financial responsibility, long-term employment, a boss, duty, success, failure, or their own bad decisions. Sheltered by family, then set free from parental oversight, they giddily enjoy their newfound freedom, and they can truly be themselves without being constrained to behave differently. That is the epitome of what the world sees as existential authenticity. Thus irresponsible, youthful spontaneity—impulsiveness—has been elevated and christened as something noble, and the perpetual adolescent is seen as the most authentic person.

Over the years since Freud, youthful authenticity has increasingly dominated the culture to such a degree that almost all advertising and entertainment is now aimed at thirteen- to twenty-four-year-olds—even though they have the least money. They're not out of their parents' basement yet, but in this postmodern culture, they define what authenticity looks like.

Evangelical mavens of "cultural engagement" see that trend, and for the past few decades they have been telling church leaders that the church must adapt to it or risk losing the next generation. The church must no longer preach against that kind of authenticity, they say, because young people have rejected the church. They see the church as an assembly of hypocrites who are not willing to be authentic—phony people playing a game. In a culture where self-centered hedonists are seen as heroic and piety is regarded as inherently fake, the church can't win adherents by preaching about holiness—or so the church-growth gurus said.

Countless church leaders seemed to find that plea persuasive. Apparently they thought it was *their* job, not God's, to get the prodigal young people back in the church. They purposely dumbed down their teaching, spiced up the atmosphere in their services, and transformed their churches into something that they thought would appeal to a frivolous, immature, adolescent culture.

The Church Courts the World's Favor

Prior to the 1960s no one expected a church service to be entertaining. No one wanted to be told to touch their neighbor and repeat a trite phrase suggested by the preacher. No one thought of worship as a physical stimulation. No one dreamed of using flashing lights and smoke to set the atmosphere in a worship service. No one demanded to be told that God accepts them just the way they are.

When you went to church you expected to be thoughtful and quiet—prayerful, sober, reflective. The service was ordered so that the word of God was central. It was read and proclaimed with the aim of leading you to understanding, conviction, transformation, and elevation. The structure was deliberate, and the objective was for people to have an encounter with God through an understanding of his truth, with an opportunity to express it in corporate worship.

But by the time large-scale protests and student rebellions came into vogue in the 1960s, some of the experts were already telling church leaders that God-centered worship, sober reverence, and serious preaching from the Bible about sin and holiness are all far too absolute, too narrow, irrelevant, and possibly even offensive to the culture in which we live. Young people were seeking "authenticity" (sin and all), and they had no interest in sanctification, holiness, purity, godliness, or separation from the world.

Because many church leaders were not well grounded in Scripture and sound doctrine themselves, they were susceptible to those ideas. They lost sight of the fact that their job was not to make unbelievers happy with the church; it was to feed and lead and guard the flock of God—and to teach the saints to be like Christ. The pragmatic philosophies they adopted eliminated any emphasis on sin, righteousness, and judgment—the very issues Jesus said the Holy Spirit would convict the world about (John 16:8–11).

There is a heretical view of sanctification that perfectly fits with such a pragmatic church-growth strategy. Historically, it's called *antinomianism*. It starts with a denial that the moral precepts of God's law remain obligatory as a rule of life for Christians. It therefore creates a radical disjunction between behavior and belief, and it erroneously uncouples sanctification from justification. This doctrine implies that the moral demands of God's law are malleable, or that they are optional, or that they have been abrogated. Indeed, some of the more extreme antinomians have openly made such claims.

Turning Grace Into Licentiousness

This is the perfect doctrine for someone who thinks existential authenticity is high virtue, because the antinomian simply says, "Hey, God saved me. I'm under grace; I don't have to worry about sin, righteousness, or judgment. This is who I am; this is how God wired me."

Antinomians abuse the principle of substitutionary atonement. It is quite true that Christ not only paid for his people's sins on the cross but he also perfectly fulfilled the law of God on their behalf. In other words, his perfect life (what theologians refer to as his "active obedience"— the righteousness of a sinless man who rendered a whole lifetime of perfect obedience to God's law) is imputed to believers. God "made him to be sin who knew no sin, so that in him we might become the righteousness of God" (2 Cor. 5:21).

The antinomian stakes his claim on that doctrine and reasons that he therefore does not need to be troubled about his own lack of obedience. Antinomians take God's forgiveness for granted (they presume on his grace), and they spurn the law as a relic of old-covenant religion. One preacher said it this way: "'Thou shalt not' does not apply to me. It's part of a covenant between God and Old Testament Israel."

Also, according to this view, if a believer must suppress an urge in order to obey the word of God out of sense of responsibility, duty, reverence, respect, or obligation, it's deemed a work of the flesh and therefore sinful.

But such an idea makes obedience and disobedience equally carnal. So who wouldn't take the easy route—perhaps even the more noble route of authenticity—and give into one's own desires? Lots of people do. One of the rules of postmodernity is that we're supposed to affirm them in their journey anyway. It's another reason sanctification gets so little mention in evangelical circles today.

Antinomianism is a very old heresy. (The term was coined by Martin Luther as a description of Johannes Agricola and other early Lutherans who were teaching that new-covenant ministers should never preach from the law.) Antinomianism dominated American evangelicalism in the mid-twentieth century, thanks to some influential theologians who argued that to highlight the lordship of Christ in connection with the gospel message was to corrupt the gospel and establish a religion based on works. That view seemed for a while to be dying, but lately it has been making a comeback in a new and revised edition that has gained popularity among young-and-restless and neo-Reformed evangelicals. They tend to regard antinomianism as a kind of noble heresy, because they see it not only as a cure for legalism, but also as a badge of authenticity.

The truth is, antinomianism and legalism are two sides of the same coin. The legalist thinks he's spiritual because he observes a law; the antinomian thinks he's spiritual because he doesn't. Both define the Christian life by *what they do with regard to the law* rather than stressing the need for the Spirit's empowerment to conform us to Christ's likeness. The legalist will never be able to restrain the flesh with his legalism (Gal. 5:17). And the antinomian who refuses even to hear the law because he thinks rules of any kind are a threat to his "liberty" is still in bondage to sin (Rom. 6:15–16). Both legalism and antinomianism are hostile to the Spirit's work in sanctification. Both the legalist and the antinomian will crash and burn.

The defining feature of a sound, biblical Christian worldview is the truth that we who believe are "in Christ" (2 Cor. 5:17). We are joined to Christ, united with him spiritually. We love Christ (1 Cor. 16:22; Eph. 6:24). We are indwelt by the Holy Spirit (John 14:17; Rom. 8:9), who empowers us, gives us true liberty from the bondage of sin, and is conforming us to the image of Christ (2 Cor. 3:17–18).

7

What Grace Teaches

Decades of antinomian influence have conditioned evangelicals to think of divine grace mainly if not exclusively in terms of forgiveness—a reprieve from the penalty of sin. That is certainly an important aspect of grace. But it's not all there is to it. *Grace* is often defined in very abridged terms as "unmerited favor." It is that, but it's much more than that. A gift given to a friend is an unearned favor. Sacrificing something of unspeakable value for the benefit of an enemy would be a better illustration of the divine grace that purchased forgiveness for sinners (Rom. 5:7–10).

Furthermore, grace is not static; Scripture describes it as an active force. Grace strengthens us (2 Tim. 2:1; Heb. 13:9); it works in us (1 Cor. 15:10); it produces faith and love in our hearts (1 Tim. 1:14); it gives us help in times of need (Heb. 4:16); and it instructs us (Titus 2:11–12).

How does grace instruct us, and what does it teach? The biblical answer to that question is a definitive refutation of antinomian doctrine: "The grace of God . . . train[s] us to renounce ungodliness and worldly passions, and to live self-controlled, upright, and godly lives" (2:12). In other words, the same grace that saves sinners from the penalty of their sin also instructs them in holiness.

Discipline

The Greek word translated "training" is *paideuō,* a word that speaks of discipline. The same word is translated "punish" in Luke 23:16, 22 and 2 Corinthians 6:9. It carries the ideas of teaching, correction, and chastening. It's the same word used for *discipline* in Hebrews 12:6: "The Lord disciplines the one he loves." It describes a process that at times "seems painful rather than pleasant, but later it yields the peaceful fruit of righteousness to those who have been trained by it" (12:11).

There's more in Titus 2. Look at the larger context. Paul tells Titus:

> The grace of God has appeared, bringing salvation for all people, training us to renounce ungodliness and worldly passions, and to live self-controlled, upright, and godly lives in the present age, waiting for our blessed hope, the appearing of the glory of our great God and Savior Jesus Christ, who gave himself for us to redeem us from all lawlessness and to purify for himself a people for his own possession who are zealous for good works. Declare

these things; exhort and rebuke with all authority. Let no one disregard you. (Titus 2:11–15)

Correction

Grace not only disciplines us for holiness' sake; it also trains us to renounce sin, and it prompts us to await eagerly the return of Christ. Why? Because "everyone who thus hopes in him purifies himself as he is pure" (1 John 3:3).

And note carefully what else Paul tells Titus: Christ died not merely to liberate us from the *penalty* of sin but also to redeem us from *lawlessness itself*—to purify us and to transform us into people who are zealous for good works. Moreover, Paul instructs Titus not to soft-sell these vital truths. He is to admonish and reprove those who are lax in receiving the sanctifying instruction of God's grace, and he is not to permit anyone to disregard the message. Paul is saying in effect, "Hammer hard on the antinomians and correct their faulty view of grace."

Power

There is one other crucial way Scripture pictures grace as dynamic rather than inert. Romans 5:21 says that grace is supposed to reign over our hearts in the same way sin once reigned. Grace is not a doormat we can casually use to wipe sin off our feet; it rules as a monarch over us.

How does grace redeem us from lawlessness and purify us? Not merely by instructing and disciplining and admonishing us "to live self-controlled, upright, and godly lives," but also by empowering us to that end. "God . . . works in you, both to will and to work for his good pleasure" (Phil. 2:13). Ultimately the Lord himself will make us stand "blameless before the presence of his glory with great joy" (Jude 24). Can I say it simply? *Sanctification is a process of fighting for full joy and not selling out for a cheap substitute along the way.*

There is of course discipline and correction in the process, but such discipline is "for our good, *that we may share his holiness*" (Heb. 12:10). The goal, again, is Christlikeness.

And that brings us back to where we began—Paul's words in Galatians 4:19: "My little children, . . . I am again in the anguish of childbirth until Christ is formed in you!"

It is not a proper goal for a pastor to hope people will be content with his messages. No pastor should imagine that the size of his congregation is a measure of his effectiveness. A godly pastor can be satisfied with nothing less than the sanctification of his people. It's a goal that will never be fully achieved until we are finally glorified.

Likewise, this is the goal each believer must keep pressing on toward. "Beloved, we are God's children now, and what we will be has not yet appeared; but we know that when he appears we shall be like him, because we shall see him as he is. And everyone who thus hopes in him purifies himself as he is pure" (1 John 3:2–3).

General Index

Scripture Index

Also Available from John MacArthur

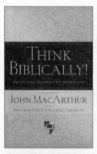

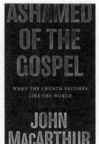

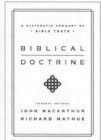

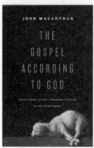

For more information, visit **crossway.org**.